Welcome to the Alpha-Bakery, where the ABC's are recipes, and the recipes are delicious. Where you and your kids can have fun together, measuring, mixing, baking and enjoying each other's company, along with the veggies, pizza, cookies and cakes.

For your kids, baking with the Alpha-Bakery is more than a matter of baking. It's helping mom prepare a meal. It's fixing a snack with dad. It's baking up a batch of goodies to take to school.

It's fun, wholesome, happy.

And, in the process, your kids develop valuable hand and eye coordination. They refine small motor skills and build reading and arithmetic skills, too.

Best of all, baking with the Alpha-Bakery helps instill confidence. Your kids develop a sense of accomplishment. They can see, taste and share, with pride, the results of their efforts.

You can make it a family affair, too. Let everyone lend a helping hand. Even cleanup can be fun when everyone pitches in.

So visit the Alpha-Bakery today, and experience all the good things that come from baking with your kids. It's a happy, wholesome way to create homemade fun!

1

TABLE OF CONTENTS PAGE

Aa is for

A a

4

Apple Crisp

4 medium unpeeled or peeled cooking apples,
   sliced (about 4 cups)
¾ cup of Gold Medal all-purpose flour
¾ cup of packed brown sugar
½ cup of quick-cooking or regular oats
⅓ cup of chopped walnuts
1½ teaspoons of ground cinnamon
½ cup of margarine or butter, softened

1. Heat the oven to 375°.
2. Spread the apple slices in an
ungreased 8-inch square pan.
3. Mix remaining ingredients with fork;
sprinkle over apples.
4. Bake uncovered until the topping is
golden brown and apples are tender,
about 30 minutes.

Makes about 6 servings.

Bb is for

B b

Banana Bread

¾ cup of sugar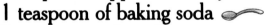
1½ cups of mashed bananas (3 large)
¾ cup of vegetable oil
2 eggs
2 cups of Gold Medal all-purpose flour
½ cup of chopped nuts, if you like
1 teaspoon of baking soda
2 teaspoons of vanilla
½ teaspoon of baking powder
½ teaspoon of salt

1. Heat the oven to 325°.
2. Grease a loaf pan, either 9x5x3 or 8½x4½x2½ inches, with shortening, using a pastry brush.
3. Mix sugar, bananas, oil and eggs in a large bowl with a wooden spoon. Stir in remaining ingredients. Pour into pan.
4. Bake until a wooden pick inserted in center of the bread comes out clean, 60 to 70 minutes. Let cool 10 minutes, then loosen sides of loaf from pan and remove from pan. Let cool completely before slicing.
Makes 1 loaf.

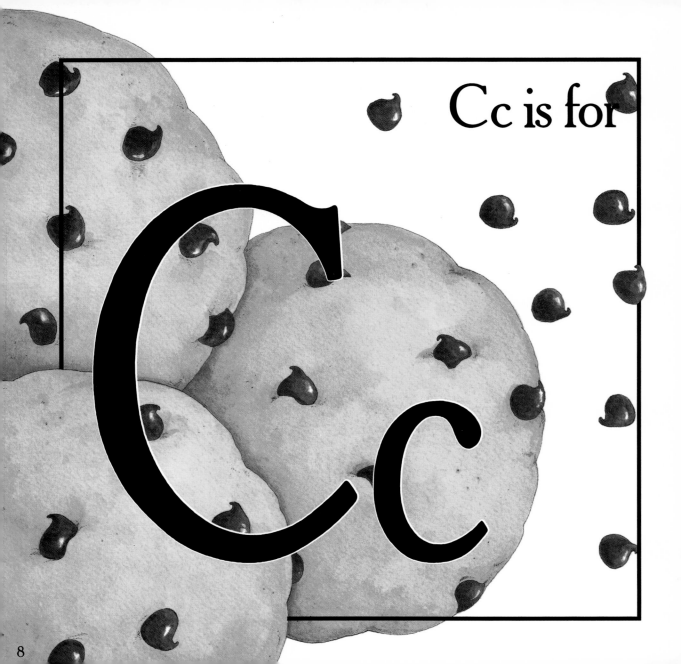

Cc is for

C c

Chocolate Chip Cookies

¾ cup of granulated sugar
¾ cup of packed brown sugar
1 cup of margarine or butter, softened
1 egg
2¼ cups of Gold Medal all-purpose flour
1 teaspoon of baking soda
½ teaspoon of salt
1 cup of coarsely chopped nuts
1 package (12 ounces) of semisweet chocolate chips (2 cups)

1. Heat the oven to 375°.

2. Mix both sugars, margarine and egg in a large bowl with a wooden spoon. Stir in flour, baking soda and salt (dough will be stiff). Stir in nuts and chocolate chips.

3. Drop dough by rounded tablespoonfuls about 3 inches apart onto an ungreased cookie sheet.

4. Bake until light brown, 8 to 10 minutes (centers will be soft). Let cookies cool slightly, then remove from cookie sheet with a spatula. Makes about 48 cookies.

Dd is for

Delicious Drumsticks

½ cup of Gold Medal all-purpose flour
1 teaspoon of salt
½ teaspoon of paprika
¼ teaspoon of pepper
6 chicken drumsticks (about 1½ pounds)
¼ cup of margarine or butter, melted and cooled

1. Heat the oven to 425°.
2. Mix flour, salt, paprika and pepper in a bowl.
3. Dip chicken drumsticks into margarine; roll in flour mixture to coat.
4. Arrange in an ungreased square pan, 8x8x2 inches.

5. Bake uncovered until juice of chicken is no longer pink when centers of thickest pieces are cut, about 50 minutes.
Makes 6 drumsticks.

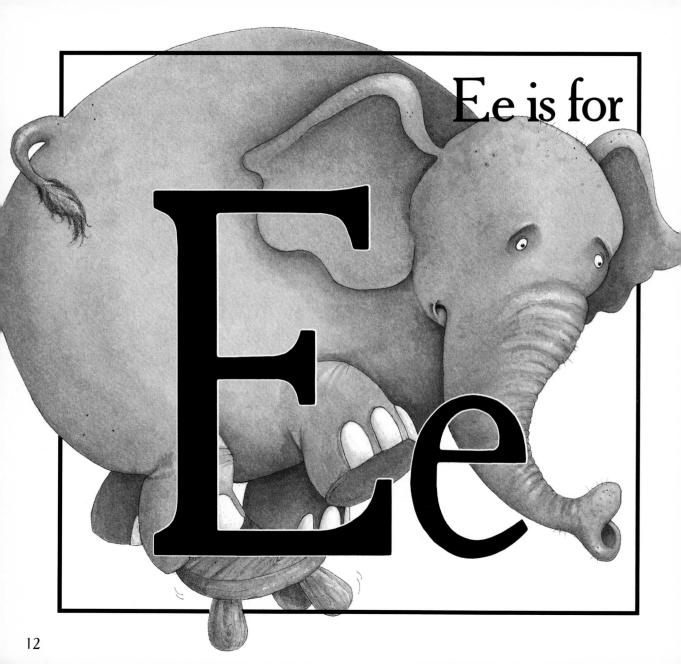

Ee is for E e

12

Elephant Ears

¼ cup of margarine or butter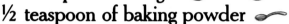
1 cup of Gold Medal all-purpose flour
2 tablespoons of sugar
½ teaspoon of baking powder
½ teaspoon of salt
⅓ cup of milk
3 tablespoons of sugar
1 teaspoon of ground cinnamon
Sugar

1. Heat the oven to 425°.
2. Grease a cookie sheet with shortening.
3. Heat margarine until melted; set aside. Stir flour, 2 tablespoons sugar, the baking powder and salt in a medium bowl. Stir in milk and 3 tablespoons of the melted margarine until dough forms.
4. Sprinkle a surface lightly with flour; turn dough onto surface. Knead 10 times. Roll dough with a rolling pin or pat with hands into a rectangle, 9x5 inches. Brush with remaining melted margarine, using a pastry brush;

sprinkle with mixture of 3 tablespoons sugar and the cinnamon.
5. Roll dough up tightly, beginning at narrow end. Pinch edge of dough into roll to seal. Cut into 4 equal pieces with sharp knife. Place cut sides up on cookie sheet; pat each into a 6-inch circle. Sprinkle with more sugar.
6. Bake until golden brown, 8 to 10 minutes. Immediately remove from cookie sheet with a spatula. Let cool on wire rack.
Makes 4 elephant ears.

13

Ff is for

Fudge Brownies

¼ cup of margarine or butter
1 package (6 ounces) of semisweet chocolate chips
¾ cup of sugar
⅔ cup of Gold Medal all-purpose flour
½ teaspoon of vanilla
¼ teaspoon of baking powder
¼ teaspoon of salt
2 eggs
½ cup of chopped nuts, if you like
½ cup of semisweet chocolate chips, if you like

1. Heat the oven to 350°.
2. Grease the bottom only of a square pan, 8x8x2 inches, with shortening.
3. Heat margarine and 1 package chocolate chips in a 2-quart saucepan over low heat, stirring constantly, until melted; remove from heat. Stir in remaining ingredients except nuts and ½ cup chocolate chips real hard with a wooden spoon until smooth.
4. Stir in nuts and chocolate chips. Spread in pan with a rubber scraper.
5. Bake until the center is set, about 30 minutes. Let brownies cool completely, then cut into 1¾x1½-inch brownies. Store brownies tightly covered.

Makes 20 brownies.

Gg is for

G g

Giant Gingerbread Kids

½ cup of sugar
½ cup of shortening
½ cup of dark molasses
¼ cup of water
¾ teaspoon of salt
¾ teaspoon of ground ginger
½ teaspoon of baking soda
¼ teaspoon of ground allspice
2½ cups of Gold Medal all-purpose flour
Raisins or currants

1. Beat sugar, shortening, molasses and water in a large bowl on low speed until blended. Beat on medium speed 1 minute. Stir in remaining ingredients except raisins.

2. Cover and refrigerate until chilled, 1 to 2 hours.

3. Heat the oven to 375°.

4. Sprinkle a cloth-covered surface lightly with flour; turn dough onto surface. Roll dough with a rolling pin until ¼ inch thick. Cut with a 5- to 8-inch gingerbread kid cutter. Lift cookies carefully with a large spatula onto an ungreased cookie sheet.

5. Decorate cookies with raisins.

6. Bake until set, 8 to 10 minutes. Let cookies cool 3 minutes, then carefully remove from cookie sheet with a spatula. Cool; decorate with frosting if you like.

Makes about eleven 5-inch or six 8-inch cookies.

Hh is for

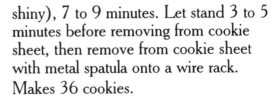

Honey Bee Cookies

½ cup of margarine or butter, softened
½ cup of packed brown sugar
½ cup of honey
1 egg
1 ½ cups of Gold Medal all-purpose flour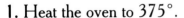
½ teaspoon of baking soda
½ teaspoon of salt
½ teaspoon of ground cinnamon

1. Heat the oven to 375°.

2. Beat margarine, brown sugar, honey and egg in a medium bowl on medium speed, scraping bowl constantly, until smooth. Stir in remaining ingredients.

3. Drop the dough by teaspoonfuls onto an ungreased cookie sheet.

4. Bake until set and light brown around edges (surfaces of cookies will appear shiny), 7 to 9 minutes. Let stand 3 to 5 minutes before removing from cookie sheet, then remove from cookie sheet with metal spatula onto a wire rack. Makes 36 cookies.

Honey-Bran Cookies: Stir 1 cup of shreds of bran cereal into batter.

Honey-Cinnamon Cookies: Mix 2 tablespoons of sugar and ½ teaspoon of ground cinnamon; sprinkle on cookies immediately after removing from oven.

Honey-Coconut Cookies: Stir 1 cup of shredded coconut into batter.

Ii is for

I i

20

Ice-cream Sandwiches

Peanut Butter Cookies (below)
About 1 pint of ice cream (any flavor), slightly softened
1 package (6 ounces) of semisweet chocolate chips
2 tablespoons of shortening

1. Bake Peanut Butter Cookies; cool.
2. For each ice-cream sandwich, press 1 slightly rounded tablespoon of ice cream between 2 cookies; place in jelly roll pan. Freeze until firm.

3. Melt chips and shortening, stirring occasionally; let stand 2 minutes. Dip half of each sandwich into chocolate. Place in pan; freeze until firm. Store wrapped in plastic wrap. Makes 15.

Peanut Butter Cookies
½ cup each of granulated sugar and packed brown sugar
½ cup of peanut butter
¼ cup each of shortening and margarine or butter, softened
1 egg
1 ¼ cups of Gold Medal all-purpose flour
¾ teaspoon of baking soda
½ teaspoon of baking powder
¼ teaspoon of salt

1. Heat the oven to 375°. Mix all ingredients. Shape into 1 ¼-inch balls.
2. Place 3 inches apart on cookie sheet.

3. Flatten in crisscross with floured fork. Bake until brown, 9 to 11 minutes.

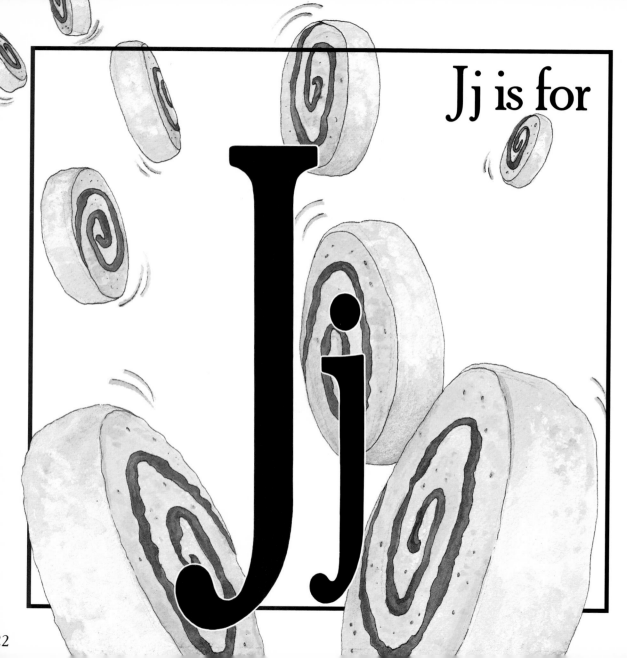

Jj is for

J j

Jelly Roll

3 eggs
1 cup of granulated sugar
⅓ cup of water
1 teaspoon of vanilla
¾ cup of Gold Medal all-purpose flour
1 teaspoon of baking powder
¼ teaspoon of salt
About ⅔ cup of jelly or jam
Powdered sugar

1. Heat the oven to 375°.
2. Line a jelly roll pan, 15½x10½x1 inch, with aluminum foil, then grease with shortening.
3. Beat eggs in a large bowl on high speed until thick and lemon color. Gradually beat in granulated sugar. Beat in water and vanilla on low speed. Gradually beat in flour, baking powder and salt until smooth. Pour into pan; spread to corners.
4. Bake until wooden pick inserted in center comes out clean, 12 to 15 minutes. Generously sprinkle

powdered sugar on a towel a little larger than the cake.
5. Immediately loosen cake from pan and turn over onto the towel. Carefully remove foil. Trim off any crisp edges of cake. While hot, carefully roll cake and towel from narrow end. Let cool on wire rack at least 30 minutes.
6. Unroll cake and remove towel. Beat jelly with a fork just enough to soften; spread over cake. Roll up cake and sprinkle with powdered sugar.
Makes 10 servings.

Kk is for

24

"Kart-Wheels"

1 ½ cups of Gold Medal all-purpose flour
½ cup of margarine or butter, softened
¼ cup of powdered sugar
½ teaspoon of baking powder
2 tablespoons of milk
About 1 cup of pie filling or jam (any flavor)

1. Heat the oven to 375°.
2. Mix flour, margarine, powdered sugar, baking powder and just enough milk until dough forms. (If dough seems dry, mix in more milk, 1 teaspoon at a time.)
3. Divide the dough into 6 equal parts. Shape each part into a ball. Place on an ungreased cookie sheet; flatten slightly. Make an indentation, 1 ¾ inches in diameter and about ¾ inch deep, in center of each flattened ball.

4. Fill each indentation with about 2 tablespoons of pie filling.
5. Bake until the edges begin to brown, 20 to 25 minutes.
Makes 6 "Kart-Wheels".

Ll is for

Lemon Squares

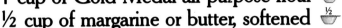

1 cup of Gold Medal all-purpose flour
½ cup of margarine or butter, softened
¼ cup of powdered sugar
1 cup of granulated sugar
2 teaspoons of grated lemon peel, if you like
2 tablespoons of lemon juice
½ teaspoon of baking powder
¼ teaspoon of salt
2 eggs

1. Heat the oven to 350°.
2. Mix thoroughly flour, margarine and powdered sugar in a small bowl. Press evenly with hands in bottom and about ⅝ inch up sides of an ungreased square pan, 8x8x2 inches. (If dough is sticky, flour fingers.) Bake 20 minutes.
3. Beat remaining ingredients in a medium bowl on medium speed until light and fluffy. Pour over hot crust.

4. Bake just until no indentation remains when touched lightly in center, about 25 minutes. Let stand until cool, then cut into about 1½-inch squares.
Makes 25 squares.

Lemon-Coconut Squares:
Prepare as directed in Lemon Squares except—stir ½ cup flaked coconut into fluffy mixture.

Mm is for

M m

Mud Pie

1 cup of granulated sugar
½ cup of margarine or butter, melted
⅓ cup of Gold Medal all-purpose flour
⅓ cup of cocoa
¼ teaspoon of salt
1 teaspoon of vanilla
2 eggs
1 cup of chopped nuts, if you like
¼ cup of fudge sauce or fudge ice-cream topping
1 cup of chilled whipping cream
2 tablespoons of powdered sugar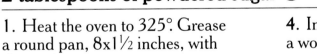

1. Heat the oven to 325°. Grease a round pan, 8x1½ inches, with shortening.

2. Mix granulated sugar, margarine, flour, cocoa, salt, vanilla and eggs in a medium bowl. Stir in nuts. Pour into pan.

3. Bake until edge appears dry and wooden pick inserted in center comes out clean (center will be moist), 35 to 37 minutes.

4. Immediately prick holes in pie with a wooden pick, then spread fudge sauce over top. Cool completely.

5. Beat whipping cream and powdered sugar in a chilled small bowl on high speed until stiff; spread over fudge sauce. Drizzle with 2 to 3 tablespoons additional fudge sauce or fudge ice-cream topping if you like. Store pie in refrigerator.
Makes 6 to 8 servings.

Nn is for

Nibble Sticks

2 cups of Gold Medal all-purpose flour
2 teaspoons of baking powder
½ teaspoon of salt
½ cup of shortening
⅔ cup of shredded Cheddar cheese
½ cup of finely chopped salami, bologna or
    fully cooked ham
About ¾ cup of milk

1. Heat the oven to 450°.
2. Mix flour, baking powder and salt in medium bowl. Cut in shortening, using pastry blender or crisscrossing 2 knives, until mixture is crumbly. Stir in cheese and salami. Stir in just enough milk so a soft dough forms.
3. Sprinkle a surface lightly with flour. Turn the dough onto the floured surface. Knead gently 10 times. Place on an ungreased cookie sheet. Pat dough into an 8-inch square; cut square in half. Cut each half crosswise into 1-inch strips.

4. Bake strips until golden, 12 to 15 minutes. Serve warm or cool with ketchup, mustard or cheese dip if you like.

Makes 16 sticks.

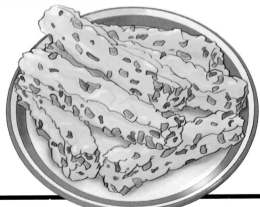

Oo is for

Oatmeal Pancakes

½ cup of Gold Medal all-purpose flour
½ cup of quick-cooking oats
¾ cup of buttermilk
¼ cup of milk
1 tablespoon of sugar
2 tablespoons of vegetable oil
1 teaspoon of baking powder
½ teaspoon of baking soda
½ teaspoon of salt
1 egg

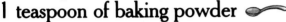

1. Beat all ingredients in a medium bowl with a hand beater until smooth. (For thinner pancakes, stir in 2 to 4 tablespoons of additional milk.)

2. Grease a heated griddle, if necessary, with shortening, using a pastry brush. (To see if griddle is hot enough, sprinkle with a few drops of water. If bubbles skitter around, heat is just right.)

3. For each pancake, pour about ¼ cup of batter onto the hot griddle.

4. Cook until pancakes are puffed and dry around edges. Turn and cook other sides until golden brown. Serve with applesauce if desired.

Makes 10 to 12 pancakes.

Pp is for

P
p

Pocket Pizza

Pizza Dough (below)
1 tablespoon of vegetable oil
¼ cup of pizza sauce
½ cup each of shredded mozzarella cheese and cooked Italian sausage
1 tablespoon of finely chopped onion
⅛ to ¼ teaspoon of garlic powder
¼ package (3-ounce size) of sliced pepperoni
2 to 3 tablespoons of pizza sauce
½ cup of shredded mozzarella cheese

1. Heat the oven to 425°. Lightly grease a cookie sheet with shortening.
2. Prepare Pizza Dough. Roll into a 12-inch circle. Fold loosely in half; place on cookie sheet and unfold. Brush with oil.
3. Layer remaining ingredients on half of the circle in order listed; fold dough over filling. Turn edge of the lower dough over edge of the top dough; pinch edge to seal. Prick top with a fork. Bake until golden brown, 20 to 25 minutes.

Pizza Dough: Beat 1 cup of Gold Medal all-purpose flour, ⅓ cup of milk, 2 tablespoons of vegetable oil, 1 teaspoon of baking powder and ½ teaspoon of salt in a bowl until the dough leaves side. Turn onto a lightly floured surface; gather into a ball. Knead 10 times. Cover with a bowl; let stand 15 minutes.

Qq is for

Quick Cheeseburger Pie

Pat-in-the-Pan Pastry (below)
1 pound of ground beef
½ to ¾ cup of finely chopped onion
1 clove of garlic, finely chopped
½ teaspoon of salt
¼ cup of Gold Medal all-purpose flour
⅓ cup of dill pickle liquid
⅓ cup of milk
½ cup of chopped dill pickles
2 cups of shredded American or Swiss cheese (8 ounces)

1. Heat the oven to 425°. Prepare pastry; pat in bottom and up sides of quiche dish, 8x2 inches, or round pan, 8x1½ inches. Bake 15 minutes.

2. Cook and stir beef, onion and garlic in 10-inch skillet until brown; drain. Sprinkle with salt and flour. Stir in pickle liquid, milk, pickles and 1 cup cheese. Spoon into dish.

3. Bake 15 minutes; sprinkle with 1 cup cheese. Bake until crust is golden brown, about 5 minutes longer.

Makes 4 to 6 servings.

Pat-in-the-Pan Pastry: Mix 1⅓ cups of Gold Medal all-purpose flour and ½ teaspoon of salt. Cut in ½ cup of shortening with a pastry blender until mixture looks like tiny peas. Sprinkle in 3 to 4 tablespoons of cold water, 1 tablespoon at a time, stirring with a fork after each addition. Mix lightly until all flour is moistened and pastry almost cleans side of bowl (add 1 to 2 teaspoons water if necessary).

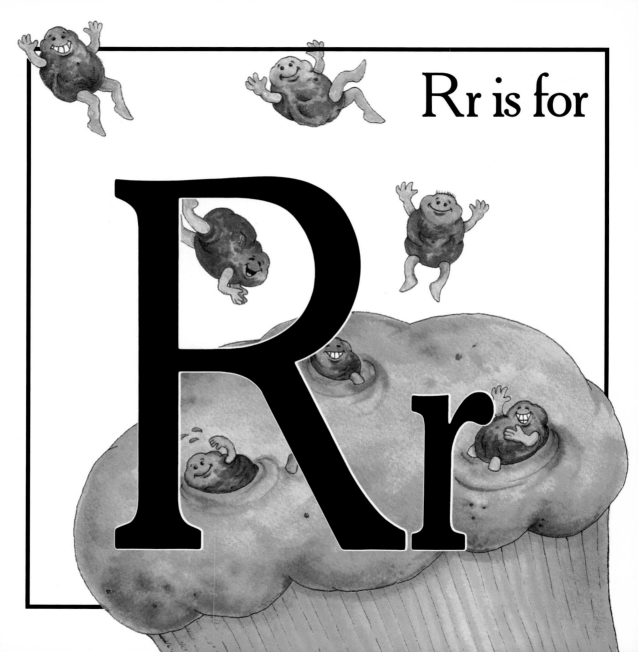

Rr is for

Raisin-Apple Muffins

1 cup of Cheerios or Apple Cinnamon Cheerios cereal, crushed
 (about ½ cup)
1 ¼ cups of Gold Medal all-purpose flour
⅓ cup of packed brown sugar
1 teaspoon of ground cinnamon
1 teaspoon of baking powder
¾ teaspoon of baking soda
⅔ cup of raisins
½ cup of applesauce
⅓ cup of milk
3 tablespoons of vegetable oil
1 egg

1. Heat the oven to 400°. Grease bottoms only of 12 medium muffin cups, 2½ x1¼ inches.

2. Mix cereal, flour, brown sugar, cinnamon, baking powder and baking soda in a large bowl. Stir in remaining ingredients just until dry ingredients are moistened.

3. Divide the batter evenly among the muffin cups.

4. Bake until golden brown, 18 to 22 minutes.
Makes 12 muffins.

39

Ss is for

S s

40

Strawberry Shortcakes

1 quart of strawberries, sliced
1 cup of sugar
2 cups of Gold Medal all-purpose flour
2 tablespoons of sugar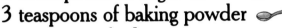
3 teaspoons of baking powder
1 teaspoon of salt
¾ cup of milk
⅓ cup of margarine or butter, melted
Sweetened Whipped Cream (below)

1. Sprinkle strawberries with 1 cup of sugar; let stand 1 hour.

2. Heat the oven to 450°.

3. Mix flour, 2 tablespoons of sugar, the baking powder and salt in a medium bowl. Stir in milk and margarine just until blended.

4. Sprinkle a surface lightly with flour. Turn the dough onto the surface. Gently smooth into a ball; knead 20 to 25 times. Roll or pat dough ¾ inch thick; cut into shortcakes with a floured 3- to 3½-inch biscuit cutter. Place on an ungreased cookie sheet.

5. Bake until golden brown, 10 to 12 minutes.

6. Split warm shortcakes crosswise; fill and top with strawberries. Serve with Sweetened Whipped Cream.

Makes 4 servings.

Sweetened Whipped Cream:

Beat 1 cup of chilled whipping cream and 2 tablespoons of powdered sugar in a chilled small bowl until stiff.

Tt is for

Turtle Bread

2½ to 3 cups of Gold Medal all-purpose flour
1 package of <u>quick-acting</u> active dry yeast
1 tablespoon of sugar
1 teaspoon of salt
½ cup of water
⅓ cup of milk
1 tablespoon of margarine or butter
1 egg
2 raisins

1. Mix 1½ cups of the flour, the yeast, sugar and salt in a large bowl.

2. Heat water, milk and margarine to 125° to 130°; stir into yeast mixture. Stir in egg. Stir in enough of remaining flour to make the dough easy to handle.

3. Sprinkle a surface lightly with flour. Turn the dough onto the surface; knead until smooth and elastic, about 5 minutes. Cover and let rest 10 minutes.

4. Lightly grease a cookie sheet. Shape a 2-inch piece of dough into a ball for head. Shape 4 walnut-size pieces of dough into balls for feet.

Shape 1 walnut-size piece of dough into tail. Shape remaining dough into a ball for body; place on cookie sheet and flatten slightly. Attach head, feet and tail by placing 1 end of each under edge of body to secure. Press raisins into head for eyes. Cover and let rise 20 minutes.

5. Heat the oven to 400°. Make crisscross cuts in body, ¼ inch deep, to look like a turtle's shell. Bake until golden brown, 20 to 25 minutes.
Makes 1 turtle bread.

Uu is for

Uu

44

Upside-down Pineapple Cake

¼ cup of margarine or butter
⅔ cup of packed brown sugar
1 can (20 ounces) of sliced pineapple, drained
Maraschino cherries, if you like
1⅓ cups of Gold Medal all-purpose flour
1 cup of granulated sugar
⅓ cup of shortening
¾ cup of milk
1½ teaspoons of baking powder
½ teaspoon of salt
1 egg

1. Heat the oven to 350°. Heat margarine in 10-inch ovenproof skillet or square pan, 9x9x2 inches, in the oven until melted.

2. Sprinkle brown sugar over margarine; arrange pineapple slices on top. Place a cherry in center of each pineapple slice.

3. Beat remaining ingredients in a large bowl on low speed 30 seconds, scraping bowl constantly. Beat on high speed 3 minutes, scraping bowl occasionally. Pour over fruit in skillet; spread evenly.

4. Bake until a wooden pick inserted in the center of the cake comes out clean, skillet 45 to 50 minutes, square 55 to 60 minutes.

5. Immediately turn the skillet upside down on a heatproof plate. Let the skillet remain over the cake a few minutes. Serve warm and, if you like, with sweetened whipped cream.

Makes 9 servings.

Vv is for

Veggie Bites

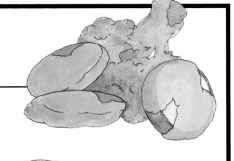

⅓ cup of margarine or butter, melted

1 egg

2 teaspoons of water

½ cup of Gold Medal all-purpose flour

½ teaspoon of salt

2 cups of fresh vegetables (broccoli flowerets or cauliflowerets, ¼-inch carrot slices, ½-inch zucchini slices, ½-inch strips green or red pepper)

1. Heat the oven to 450°. Brush bottom of rectangular pan, 13x9x2 inches, with about 1 tablespoon of the melted margarine.

2. Beat egg and water with a fork in a shallow dish. Mix flour and salt in another shallow dish.

3. Dip about ¼ of the vegetables into egg mixture. Remove 1 vegetable piece at time with a slotted spoon, fork or hands; roll in flour mixture to coat. Place in pan.

4. Repeat with remaining vegetables. Pour remaining margarine carefully over each vegetable piece and into pan.

5. Bake uncovered, turning once, until vegetables are crisp-tender and coating is golden brown, 10 to 12 minutes; drain. Sprinkle lightly with grated Parmesan cheese if you like.

Makes 2 cups of vegetable bites.

Ww is for

Wonderful Waffles

1 cup of Gold Medal all-purpose flour
2 teaspoons of baking powder
1 teaspoon of sugar
¼ teaspoon of salt
1 cup of milk
¼ cup of margarine or butter, melted
1 egg, separated

1. Heat the waffle iron.

2. Mix flour, baking powder, sugar and salt in a medium bowl. Stir in milk, margarine and egg yolk until blended.

3. Beat egg white in a small bowl on high speed until stiff peaks form; fold flour mixture into egg white.

4. Pour about ⅔ cup of the batter onto center of the hot waffle iron. Bake until steaming stops. Remove waffle carefully. Repeat with remaining batter. Makes three 8-inch waffles.

Xx is for

"Xtra-Special" Celebration Cake

3 cups of Gold Medal all-purpose flour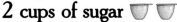
2 cups of sugar
½ cup of cocoa
2 teaspoons of baking soda
1 teaspoon of salt
⅔ cup of vegetable oil
2 teaspoons of vinegar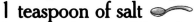
1 teaspoon of vanilla
2 cups of cold water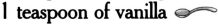
1 tub (16 ounces) of ready-to-spread frosting (any flavor)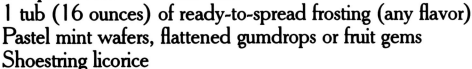
Pastel mint wafers, flattened gumdrops or fruit gems
Shoestring licorice

1. Heat the oven to 350°. Grease 2 round pans, 9x1 ½ inches; dust with flour.
2. Mix flour, sugar, cocoa, baking soda and salt in a large bowl.
3. Mix oil, vinegar and vanilla. Stir oil mixture and water into flour mixture real hard until well blended, about 1 minute. Immediately pour batter into pans, dividing evenly.
4. Bake until wooden pick inserted in center comes out clean, about 35 minutes; let cool 10 minutes.
5. Remove from pans; let cake cool completely. Fill and frost cake as directed on frosting tub. Arrange wafer "balloons" on top of cake; use licorice to make balloon strings.

Yy is for

Y y

52

Yogurt Cups

¾ cup of Gold Medal all-purpose flour
¼ cup of margarine or butter, softened
3 tablespoons of powdered sugar
2 to 3 teaspoons of cold water
1⅓ cups of yogurt (any flavor)

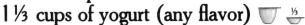

1. Heat the oven to 375°.
2. Mix flour, margarine and powdered sugar until crumbly; sprinkle in water, 1 teaspoon at a time, stirring until dough forms.
3. Press about 3 tablespoons of dough in bottom and up side of each of 4 ungreased 6-ounce custard cups to within ½ inch of top.
4. Bake until golden brown, 10 to 12 minutes; let cool 10 minutes. *Carefully* remove from cups with a small metal spatula; let cool completely on wire rack.

5. Fill each cup with ⅓ cup of yogurt; garnish with fresh fruit if you like.
Makes 4 cups.

Zz is for

Zebra Cookies

3 cups of Gold Medal all-purpose flour
1 cup of granulated sugar
²⁄₃ cup of powdered sugar
1 teaspoon of vanilla
1 ¼ cups of margarine or butter, softened
¼ teaspoon of salt
1 egg
¼ cup of cocoa

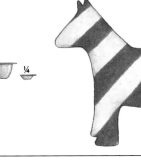

1. Mix flour, both sugars, vanilla, margarine, salt and egg until dough forms. Divide dough into halves. Mix cocoa into 1 half.

2. Sprinkle a surface very lightly with flour. Pat or roll each half of dough on the floured surface into a 9-inch square. Cut each square into three 3-inch strips. Cut strips crosswise into halves.

3. Lift 1 brown strip half with large metal spatula and place on plastic wrap. Top with 1 white strip half; press firmly. Top with remaining 10 brown and white strip halves, alternating colors and pressing layers firmly to form into a bar, about 4½ inches long, 3 inches wide and 3 inches high.

Wrap in plastic wrap and refrigerate until chilled, 1 to 2 hours.

4. Heat the oven to 375°. Cut bar of dough crosswise into about eighteen ¼-inch slices. Cut each slice with floured horse-shaped cookie cutter, about 3x2 inches.* Place on an ungreased cookie sheet.

5. Bake cookies until edges begin to brown, 8 to 10 minutes. Let cookies cool slightly, then remove from cookie sheet with a spatula.

Makes about 18 cookies.

*Or if you like, cut each slice crosswise in half instead of using a cookie cutter. Makes about 36 cookies.

Fun with dough!

Creative Dough

1 cup of Gold Medal all-purpose flour
2 teaspoons of cream of tartar
½ teaspoon of salt
1 cup of water
1 tablespoon of vegetable oil
1 teaspoon of vanilla, if you like
About 15 drops of your favorite food color

1. Cook all ingredients in 1½-quart saucepan over medium heat, stirring real hard, about 4 minutes or until mixture forms a ball.

2. Remove from saucepan and let stand on counter 5 minutes.

3. Knead dough about 30 seconds or until it is smooth and blended. Cool completely. Store in airtight container in refrigerator.

Fun with paper!

Papier-Mâché

2 cups of cold water 🥛🥛
1½ to 1¾ cups of Gold Medal all-purpose flour 🥛 ½ ¼
Newspaper, cut into strips that measure about
    1x15 inches

1. Mix water and flour in large bowl with wire whisk until smooth. Mixture should be the same thickness as heavy cream.

2. Coat a mold* with one layer newspaper strips which have been dipped in water. Then dip strips in flour mixture and lay over first layer of strips until mold is well coated.

3. Let stand until strips on mold are dry and hard. Paint over the strips if you like.

*Molded clay or an inflated balloon makes a good mold.

Finger Paint

⅓ cup of cornstarch
3 tablespoons of sugar
2 cups of cold water
Food color

1. Mix cornstarch, sugar and water in 1-quart saucepan.

2. Cook and stir over medium heat about 5 minutes or until thickened; remove from heat.

3. Divide the mixture into separate cups or containers. Tint mixture in each container with a different food color. Stir several times until cool. Store in an airtight container. (The paint works best if you use it the same day you make it.)

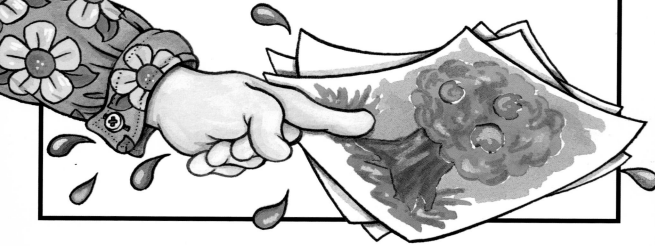

Crispy Cereal Cookies

1 cup of margarine or butter, softened
1 cup of granulated sugar
⅔ cup of packed brown sugar
2 eggs, beaten
1 teaspoon of vanilla
½ cup of peanut butter
2 cups of Gold Medal all-purpose
    or unbleached flour
1 teaspoon of baking powder
1 teaspoon of baking soda
½ teaspoon of salt
4 cups of Cheerios cereal
1½ cups of candy-coated chocolate candies

1. Heat the oven to 350°.
2. Mix margarine and both sugars in a large bowl. Stir in eggs, vanilla and peanut butter until well blended.
3. Mix flour, baking powder, baking soda and salt. Stir flour mixture into margarine mixture. Stir in cereal and candies.

4. Drop the dough by rounded teaspoonfuls onto an ungreased cookie sheet.
5. Bake until golden brown, 8 to 10 minutes. Cool 1 minute, then remove from cookie sheet with a spatula. Cool on a wire rack.
Makes about 6½ dozen cookies.

Jungle Fun Toss

2 cups of Apple Cinnamon Cheerios cereal

2 cups of Cheerios cereal

2 cups of Honey Nut Cheerios cereal

1½ cups of animal crackers

1½ cups of pretzel twists

1½ cups of cheese-flavored snack crackers

½ cup of assorted Betty Crocker or Fruit Corners chewy fruit
   snack shapes or gummi candy shapes

1. Mix all ingredients in a large bowl.
2. Store in an airtight container.
Makes 10½ cups snack.

Confetti Caramel Corn

7 cups of Trix cereal
⅓ cup of packed brown sugar
⅓ cup of margarine or butter
2 tablespoons of light corn syrup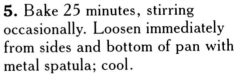
1 teaspoon of vanilla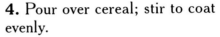
¼ teaspoon of baking soda

1. Heat the oven to 300°. Place cereal in a jelly roll pan, 15½x10½x1 inch.

2. Mix brown sugar, margarine and corn syrup in a 1½-quart saucepan. Heat mixture over medium heat about 3 minutes, stirring occasionally, until margarine is melted and mixture begins to boil. Cook, without stirring, 4 minutes longer. (Mixture will boil and turn golden brown.) Remove from heat.

3. Stir in vanilla and baking soda until mixture is foamy.

4. Pour over cereal; stir to coat evenly.

5. Bake 25 minutes, stirring occasionally. Loosen immediately from sides and bottom of pan with metal spatula; cool.

Makes about 7 cups snack.

Warning: Brown sugar mixture will be very hot—handle carefully.

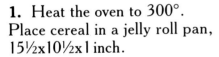

Lucky Charms® Cutouts

1 cup of peanut butter chips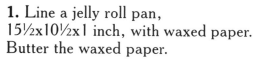
1 cup of vanilla milk chips
½ cup of light corn syrup
3 tablespoons of margarine or butter
7 cups of Lucky Charms cereal
Cookie cutters (star, moon, clover, horseshoe,
   balloon, heart and diamond shapes are fun)

1. Line a jelly roll pan, 15½x10½x1 inch, with waxed paper. Butter the waxed paper.

2. Heat peanut butter chips, vanilla chips, corn syrup and margarine in a 3-quart or larger saucepan over medium heat, stirring constantly, until melted. Remove from heat.

3. Stir in cereal until evenly coated. Press in pan with buttered back of a spoon. Refrigerate about 20 minutes or until slightly firm.

4. Cut cereal mixture into desired shapes with cookie cutters (or into 2x1½-inch bars). Roll remaining cereal mixture into balls, about 1½ inches. Cover and refrigerate any remaining charms up to 3 days.

Makes about 19 charms (2½ inches) and 17 balls or 50 bars.

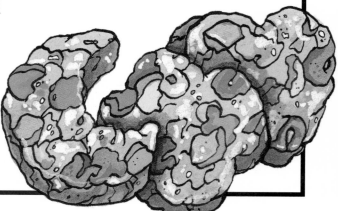

Sticks and Stones Snack

4 cups of Kix cereal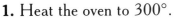
2 cups of pretzel sticks
⅓ cup of margarine or butter, melted*
¼ teaspoon of Worcestershire sauce
2 cups of raisins

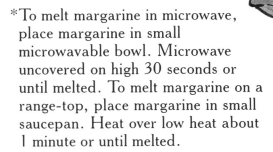

1. Heat the oven to 300°.

2. Mix cereal and pretzel sticks in an ungreased rectangular pan, 13x9x2 inches.

3. Stir margarine and Worcestershire sauce in a small bowl. Pour over cereal mixture, tossing until evenly coated.

4. Bake uncovered 25 minutes, stirring occasionally.

5. Stir in raisins. Cool. Store in an airtight container.

Makes about 8 cups snack.

*To melt margarine in microwave, place margarine in small microwavable bowl. Microwave uncovered on high 30 seconds or until melted. To melt margarine on a range-top, place margarine in small saucepan. Heat over low heat about 1 minute or until melted.

Alpha-Bakery   Kitchen Tips

Directions for proper measurement of ingredients

For successful cooking, measure accurately using utensils appropriate for dry and liquid ingredients.

Margarine or Butter—For butter in stick form, cut desired amount (each stick equals ½ cup or 8 tablespoons.) For butter in block form, soften and pack firmly in nested measuring cup; level and remove with rubber spatula.

Glass Measuring Cup—Use to measure liquids. Always read the measurement at eye level.

Gold Medal All-Purpose Flour—Spoon lightly into nested measuring cup; level with metal spatula.

Graduated Measuring Spoons—Use to measure

liquids and dry ingredients. For thin liquids, pour into spoon until full.

Graduated Nested Measuring Cups—Use to measure dry ingredients and solid fats.

Milk (and other thin liquids)—Pour into glass measuring cup; check amount at eye level.

Molasses (and thick liquids)—Pour into glass measuring cup; check amount at eye level and remove contents with rubber spatula.

Shortening—Pack firmly in nested measuring cup; level and remove with rubber spatula.

Shredded Cheese (also soft crumbs, raisins and nuts)—Pack lightly in nested measuring cup until full.

Sugar—For brown sugar, pack firmly in nested measuring cup; level with metal spatula. For granulated sugar, dip nested measuring cup into bag or canister; level with metal spatula. For powdered sugar, spoon lightly into nested measuring cup; level with metal spatula (press through sieve to remove lumps if necessary).

Vanilla (and other flavorings)—Pour into measuring spoon until full.

More Ideas to help you and your students bake successfully.

Heating the Oven—When a recipe states the oven temperature at the beginning of the cooking method, it means the oven should be heated when preparation begins. It is necessary to heat the oven for many baked items, such as breads and cakes, and also for foods that cook quickly, such as cookies and toasted nuts.

Kitchen Safety—Young children require careful supervision in the kitchen. Sharp knives, hot pans and electrical appliances can be dangerous if used or handled incorrectly. Children should be properly supervised and instructed in the correct use of kitchen utensils and appliances.

INDEX

INDEX

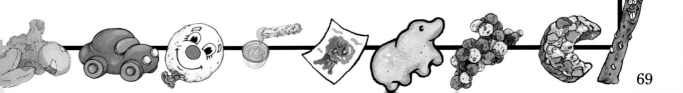

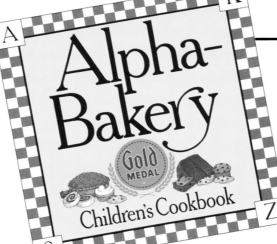

Share the fun!

The Alpha-Bakery Cookbook is a great way to share the ABC's of kitchen creativity with friends and family.

- Give the Alpha-Bakery Cookbook as a birthday or holiday gift.
- Send a copy to school for your child's teacher.
- Hand them out as party favors.

To order additional copies of the Alpha-Bakery Children's Cookbook, send $2.00 for each copy to:

Gold Medal Alpha-Bakery Children's Cookbook
P.O. Box 5119
Minneapolis, MN 55460-5119
Please allow 6 to 8 weeks for delivery.

Please send me _____ Alpha-Bakery Cookbook(s). For each cookbook ordered, I've enclosed $2.00. My check or money order made payable to General Mills is for a total of $_____.

Name _____

Address _____ Apt. _____

City _____ State _____ Zip Code _____

Send to: Gold Medal Alpha-Bakery Cookbook
P.O. Box 5119
Minneapolis, MN 55460-5119

Be sure to include zip code to ensure proper delivery. Please allow up to eight weeks for shipment. Offer good only in U.S.A. Offer good in all states except where prohibited, taxed or regulated. Offer good only while supplies last. **Offer expires Dec. 31, 2001.**